AF613996

# Orange Is the Color of Fall

Lulu Author



ISBN: 978-1-257-11058-2

This book contains selected poems

I wrote during 2010, you will find

them thought provoking as you

browse through the selections:

free verses on math, nature, or

life in general will genuinely entertain

YOU…

Great Big thanks go to my family

members for letting me float among

literature both online and in print,

words of encouragement from

fellow friends are appreciated here.

# Orange Is the Color of Fall

## Orange-**Poetry Acrostics**

Orange is the color of Fall,

Radiant and reflective to all,

As time goes by,

No doubt of its beauty or why.

Gaze into the orange sky,

Exhibit Excellence in life and fly.

## Since U R an Online Image

U look young and pretty,

U smile all over me,

Your words pour like honey,

U make my heart beat like a bunny.

I won't fall, trust me,

since u r an online image.

## Life Is No Fun without Z-Geometry

X-axis is lonely,

Y-axis is lovely;

When two of them form a right angle,

They build a plane, solid like a triangle.

X-Y plane is strong but flat,

Soon they begin to dream of something

 more than that;

Z-axis is lonely,

XY-plane is lovely,

When three of them form a family,

They constitute a space in geometry.

Thus, X-axis is cute,

XY-plane is cuter,

and X-Y-Z cubic space is the cutest.

Please look at the graphs above,

Enjoy a good laugh!

Life is no fun without Z,

You've got to learn you a-b-c!

## ABC Poem

A small bowl of cereal with fat free milk,

Brings energy to rest of the day,

Can you resist this?

Don't shy away,

Enjoy life's bliss, please!

## Via a Child's Eyes - Haikus

To live and engage,

one must break the door of the cage

and digest the words of the sage.

.

Via a child's detective eyes,

We invent magic and vampires,

Creativity shall win over sins.

## It's Winter in My City

It's winter in my city,

My cat gives birth to a kitty.

Mother cat loves her kitten

and enjoys milk in the kitchen.

Baby cat makes curious stare

Whenever her mom goes out to

breathe some fresh air.

They have fun cuddling on a rocking chair,

Watching trees trembling, lonely and bare.

## Yesterday I Took a Wrong Turn

Yesterday,

I took a wrong turn

and ended up on a cliff;

Today,

I plan my path before I start,

I accomplish things with firm belief.

Tomorrow,

I'll bury all of the sorrows

and let go of errors,

I 'll know when to stop

and orchestra my way to the top.

## Reflections and Expectations

No matter what I do,

All that I really care

is 4 words to ring true

and things to be fair.

No matter what I preach,

All that I truly enjoy

is the waves that ebb the beach

and mountain views that echo joy.

No matter what I write,

All that I genuinely love

is 4 the truth to stick out and shine bright

and stars to twinkle above.

Comb the messy hair,

Buckle your seat belt, evade no where,

Stop knocking out the wedges,

Ready, set, go, turn the pages.

## Paradise

Above the ocean,

Below the Heaven,

There is a paradise

where you can act divine or wise.

Everything will be perfect there,

You won't be bothered by subjective stare.

You can enjoy life as you will,

and let your fears roll down the hill.

There will be no accusations,

There will be no painful communications,

You simply enjoy pure minded friends,

The joy of writing and sharing has no ends.

Sorrows vanish like summer rain,

Sickness desert you without pills of pain,

The air will smell like a fresh rose,

Inspirations fill you with perfect prose…

## Say Cheese

Say cheese,

Capture the juicy smiles on your face,

Let passion and enthusiasm take place,

Demonstrate a manifesto to grow grace.

To educate, give to charity,

Showcase leadership capacity

in silence,

Not to object, but to accept life's excellence.

## I Saw an Angle in My Room Today

I saw an angle in my room today,

Her gown was pink and grey;

She smelled sweet

with magical glow under her feet.

I saw an angel in my room today,

Her hair was sparkling brown;

She brought in a soft breeze,

and some magical tricks to grace my place.

## Love Seesaw

From a mother to her child =>

It's magical time of the year,

I love you, my dear,

Light up, smile, carry no fear!

From a child to one's mother =>

Hold me tight,

Feed my soul with love and light,

Smiles, carry pride.

## Where Nature and I Become One

Following the plan,

Under the Spring sun,

I arrived at a mountain park,

where nature and I become one.

Directed by a trial map,

I began walking uphill, non-stop,

Once in a while,

I pause to break, staring at rocks in a pile.

I took photos to capture the views below,

A lake, parked cars, driving path are in view.

I would look up

2 see how far I was from the mountain top.

.

There are moments of confusions,

There are sentiments of hesitations,

"Keep Walking",

I hear my inner voice talking.

.

Near the highest spot,

I spied a young couple walking above,

Their body gesture showed their love,

How long I had been going up, I forgot.

.

When t is all the way up hill,

It is against my natural will.

After I eventually conquer the obstacles,

I believed that these were miracles.

The mountain is half bare,

Prairie dogs make their stare.

Wild cows walk wild walks,

Naughty hares talk Happy talks…

## Fishy No More

The basketball game's on,

Life's guidance gone,

Get drowned.

Whistles blow,

A free throw,

Faces glow.

Steal, dribble, score,

Fishy no more,

Win by 4.

## When It Comes 2 Math

When it comes to math,

Some fear it to death,

Some fall out of breath;

Here is a simple confess:

Math is not something worse

than giving birth…

Math is cool

if you know the rule;

Math is fun

if you are its fan.

Keep trying.

You can do it without dying…

1+1=2,

Math says something perfectly true;

2+2=4,

It's good when you make a perfect score;

3+3=6,

You've got to enjoy mathematical tricks;

If you truly understand,

You will love math and feel grand.

## Pink Grace With Faith

I love both faith and grace,
They take me many a place
And make my day a true bliss.

In a dancing way,
They fill me with pride
and keep me stay inside.

I enjoy spending time home,
reading many an online poem,
Faith is the catalyst of grace.

## There Is No Right or Wrong

Spouses cry

2 see houses fly;

Kids scream

2 see spider-man cheer for a football game;

The Sun blinks with guilt

when stones start to melt;

Goats float

as ghosts hide under a boat,

Socks talk

while robots stalk;

Dogs quack

when cats bark;

Snake

refuses to go naked near a lake;

Lover cheats

on Valentine gifts or treats…

February is frightful

because weirdness wins,

You've got to be watchful

when a rock grins.

Nothing is as solid as the stone,

Everything carries some tricky tone.

There is NO right or wrong,

Anything could go deadly crazy in town.

## Without Laughter, Life Is A…

Without leaves,

Trees stand bare;

Without beliefs,

Minds don't care.

Without gasoline,

Cars go nowhere;

Without discipline,

Chaos is everywhere.

Without water,

The earth will be dry;

Without air,

Living beings will die.

Without the sun,

No growth will be done;

Without the moon,

Stars will twinkle with a dull tune.

Without laughter,

Life is a disaster;

Without craziness,

Life becomes meaningless.

## 2 Me, Love Is Magical

To me, love is magic,

Without love, life is a tragic;

Wonders come from passions,

They are the fuel to chemical reactions.

Miracles are born from confidence,

They r awards to intelligence and prudence,

Wizardry is really a fantasy,

It is a creation of your dreams, I say.

Life could be magical,

if you keep loving, and behaving logical…

## He Gave Me His Heart

He gave me his heart

as we played hide and seek in the park,

"L LOVE YOU."

His words was sweet and true.

We would kill the day

like a ship on a bay,

Romantic thoughts kept fly our way,

It was hard not to think and pray.

Then his Dad died in a war,

His Mom left to live aboard.

I see him no more,

Life suddenly becomes dull.

I feel the pain,

I see it happen,

I fight to have our relation maintain,

But it is not the same all of a sudden.

Love is fragile,

Love is uncertain,

He gave me his heart,

Yet we fell apart.

## Sunday Keeps Me Busy

Sunday keeps me busy:
Sunday 160 is cute to play,
Potluck plus Poetry Pantry
are too delicious to betray.
Poems fly like dumplings,
I enjoy Sunday Scrabbling(s).

## I Love Morning

I love sunrise,

The time when night removes her gown

and slips away

2 date Mr. Brown.

It's No surprise

that doors open to welcome grace,

with the treatment of fresh air,

The world revolves in significant grace.

I LOVE MORNING,

It's fun to see the day start smiling.

Everything looks great

waiting for night to be back from her date.

## Moods R like Dark Woods

Moods are like dark woods,

They fancy you and frighten you.

Your feelings get hurt

when something unpleasant is said.

Emotions are like vast oceans,

You survive

only if you know how to surf and dive.

Moods, feelings, and emotions

are born from tensions.

Take charge of your mental drive,

Smile, feel happy, give me a high five!

## I Like Nike Shoes

I love Nike Shoe,

that are either yellow,

or Blue!

As bright as light,

As precious as pride,

Nike shoes fit my taste perfectly right.

## H Is 4 Hello

Hello, green earth,

Keep providing and loving,

Hello, dancing winds,

Keep those leaves singing and laughing,

Hello, chirping birds,

Keep your elegance alive by flying,

Hello, twinkling stars,

Keep your curiosity shining and inspiring,

Hello, everything in the universe,

Stay active and positive..

Happy Living!

## K Is 4 Kindness

It can't be held in hand,

Yet it makes you feel grand.

It comes all of a sudden,

and deserts you forgotten.

Tears and joy mixed,

As it hits, friendships fixed.

## Still Is a Feel That Is Real

Not as hard as steel,

Not as bad as steal,

Still is a feel

which is real.

.

When everything else is still,

One feels chill,

Your mind starts to do wonders,

Wild noises would knock against your will.

.

As if the world turns silent,

Nothing but your heartbeats heard,

As if the minutest cell runs violent,

Everything else feels dead but your head.

When everything else is still,

Your hearts runs up the hill.

It's hard to tell exactly how you feel,

You creative onion simply starts to peel.

## T-Storms Butterfly the Nature

T-storms butterfly the nature,

make rainbows in the sky,

Evoking magic in many a creature,

and imagination flickers like a butterfly.

Trees stand elegantly, smiling,

Geese stare at the sun, thinking

they are cleaner.

Cars make splashes, saying,

Look, the grass is greener.

Moon with romantic eyes, recalling

the past of the world, the dancing

feet, the disc music, evening

secrets, the whispers, breathe taking!

T-storms butterfly the nature,

Nature is invincible,

Hope is unkillable!

## W is 4 Wishes, M is 4 Magic

I wish a dream joyful and true,

I wish a day sunny and anew.

I wish a poem being deliciously done,

I wish a relation healthy and fun.

I wish a car comfortable and cool,

I wish a home loving and due.

To wish is meant to cherish,

Not to diminish.

To wish an error forgiven,

To wish a deed undone,

Take caution,

Make a wise decision,

4 the universe is ONE.

Magic is divine,

But only love, forgiveness,

and imagination lead to it,

Sign!

## It is Just A Bad Dream

I have sore shoulders,

I have itchy toes,

I have high fever,

I have running nose.

I need immediate medical care,

Shall I call 911? I suppose.

But which treatment shall I get,

My goodness, it is hard to choose.

My eyes are wet,

My hair is loose,

My phone is dead,

My credit cards confuse.

My life ends up in despair,

Shall I call 911? I suppose.

How can I survive and feel fair?

Only the divine knows.

In a frightful mood,

I run wild in the neighborhood,

I yell,

I tell…

It is just a bad dream,

I wake up

and enjoy my blissful life all the same.

## You Rock

You rock,

You work until dark.

You rule,

You are truly cool.

You write,

You do your work with pride.

You stay up late,

You feel great.

You learn,

You love what you earn.

You share,

You have gifts to spare.

You laugh,

You stand up as tall as a giraffe.

You are smart,

You cherish everything you’ve got.

## Frogs Follow Fish in a Pond

Frogs follow fish in a pond,

Forests find friends in camping ground.

Fairies fly high,

Farmers are fond of fruit pie.

Families fight to stay fit,

Film fans r feverish to famous fellows' wit.

Fall in love with fascinating Fall,

Fear nothing at all.

Facts and factors form a riddle,

Face a fabulous fiddle.

Faith facilitates fulfilling future,

Fire all the filthy creature,

Free fictional fears,

Fix fidget tears and wears.

File a final and fateful divorce

to all false and frightful force.

No more grades of F,

Enough talks of F…

## What I Write Is What I Like

I like girls smart and small,

I like boys brave and tall.

I like babies who don't squall,

I like kittens that curl up like a ball.

I like to walk in a shopping mall,

I like to listen to music in a concert hall.

I like to be as innocent as a doll,

I like to celebrate the season of Fall.

Summer is fine with solid green,

The sweetest season is spring,

Fall is perfect, I mean,

Winter is O. K. with silver sheen.

What I write

is what I like,

What I like

is what I write.

## How Men and Women Love

A woman loves a man,

She shows it via her cooking,

A man loves a woman,

He cares more about her looking.

A woman loving a man wants a child or two,

It is a bliss if the man wants the same too.

After they work out plans to stay merry,

They will get engaged and marry.

She loves him, body and soul,

He loves her, more than he can tell.

It's his greatest joy to plow and sow

As their love continue to grow.
Their baby may have Daddy's eyes,
Black, brown, or blue,
Their kitchen may have Mommy's pies,
Warm, fresh, and cool.
The loving birds know happiness
 there is no transcending,
Their marriage holds
for goodness' sake a rather cheery ending!
How women and men love,
That's my take from above.

## My Will is Strong

It's time to go,

My instincts tell me so,

I will be out of town,

I won't be able to answer your phone.

When love comes to an end,

Time to bid farewell, my friend;

My will is strong,

I must be left alone!

Stop the unrealistic expectation,

Nobody will believe your exaggeration.

Please don't ask why,

It's time to say GOODBYE!

## Blame My Vocabulary

Many times I wonder in my head

Why I do what I do,

Do people care about what I've said?

The choice of words I pull

out of my word bank has occurred

2 ring true,

How do they impact you,

I have No clue!

In case my use of words seem chary,

Blame my vocabulary.

## Fret No More

As illusions get shattered,

Nothing seems really mattered,

ideas are gathered,

concepts and terms are re-measured.

Fret no more,

Fight no more,

A war ends,

Bliss 4 families and friends.

## The Ugly Is Beautiful

On the immense ocean

Where waves shimmer under moonlight,

A beast is having a celebration:

He is a groom with pride.

He was born ugly,

He falls in love with a maiden fish

Looking lovely.

Subjective barriers do have effects at first,

She tamed him

while he wooed her with a dove;

She is all smiles to see him at his best,

He is the champion of true love.

The ugly is beautiful,

Their love is blissful.

The wedding is successful,

The crowd is wonderful.

What a harvest of passion in the sea,

This legend is encouraging enough

4 the world to see.

On the immense ocean

Where waves shimmer under moonlight,

A beast is having a celebration,

He is a groom with pride…

## Here I Am Holding a Rose

I feel un-cool

that I have ever hurt you.

I want to grab the washcloth of remorse

And wipe my soul for regeneration;

I want to take hold of the garden hose

2 enable the mending of our relation.

I want to be morning dew,

I want to be the one with you,

I want to be a butterfly,

I want to be a…, you try.

Footsteps of errors may becloud our soul,

Soap of repentance shall save the show.

Armed with regrets in the core,

I hope to rediscover my peaceful shore.

Here I ‘m holding a rose,

Take it and accept my remorse.

## They Fall Apart

Happy together they have been,

Never expected separation in between;

All of a sudden, Poisonous seed surges,

Divergence of opinions emerges,

With no beg of pardon,

No concern of their children,

and no thoughtfulness on their garden.

They fall apart,

Leaving behind many a broken heart;

When Love loses its sheen,

Wounds are too deep to amend!

**Lovely Bubbles**

Lasting only 4 a few seconds,
They glow with a rainbow light.
Stirring up excitement in the air,
What a magical transformation in sight.

Lovely bubbles, lonely bubbles,
Colorful bubbles, plain bubbles,
All dance with joy everywhere,
It's phenomenon to see them appear.

Bubbles of dreams at times
hold the envision of the bursting foam,

Discover your own rhymes,

Bring your bubbles home.

## Everyone Makes Mistakes

Signs are tools

To keep u from getting into troubled pools,

Be aware and use the clues.

Everyone makes mistakes,

That doesn't mean your life flushed in risks,

Get up and move on, no shames.

Don't tease someone's blemish,

Focus on positivist and make good use of it,

Let love and embrace flourish!

## C It Your Way

U only live your life once,

U shall not allow opportunities to go waste.

C it your way,

Make your day.

C is 4 COURAGE, the courage

2 fight anything that means to discourage.

If u r innocent,

U shall fear nothing

that r set up

2 shut u up;

If u r decent,

U shall fear nothing

that means to quiet u down

or make u drown.

U shall have the courage

not to compromise your reputation,

2 conquer possible deconstruction,

the courage to confront crimes,

2 compose poetry that rhymes.

2 collect wisdom,

2 crash boredom,

2 clarify confusions,

2 count contributions.

2 correct wrongs,

2 compile songs.

2 crack cases,

2 convey graces.

2 connect poets,

2 contest doubts,

U shall have the courage to cry,

2 try,

2 continue

your avenue

2 live, love,

and rise above…..

C it your way,

Never waste one single day.

## What Can U See?

Writers write,

Feel free to decide.

Look at the blue image of the sea,

What do u see?

I see a snow bear

with NO hair;

I see a hole

with a plastic pole;

I see a sir

Who makes a curious stare;

I see a prank

inside a water tank…

wow, come on,

Let's write about our own life song.

any questions? Ask Derik,

Enjoy the fun, No panic!

## Love Has Wings

She stares at him,

Her face wet,

With the room light dim,

He is what she wants to get.

He stares back at her,

his mind sings,

Bliss is eventually here,

Love has wings.

Body and soul,

They emerge.

Time freezes

in steaming hot breezes.

## Nobody Shall Ask U 2 Stop

When it comes to arithmetic,

1 plus 1 is equal to 2,

The equality is perfectly true.

when it comes to opinions at a poll,

1 plus 1 may not be equal to 2,

YES may be canceled by NO.

Equality reflects life's quality,

One shall be aware of conflicts in reality.

Equality in life is everyone's dream,

That's how M. L. K. won his fame.

When it comes to blogging,

Everyone has the freedom in posting.

It does not matter where you live,

It does not matter what you believe,

Your RIGHT to blog is there,

An equal opportunity for all to share.

Nobody shall ask you to stop,

Nobody shall act like a blogging cop.

Do your own share,

Never threat or scare…

Writing posts is like driving your own car,

do it with care,

near or far,

Enjoy your ride with zero despair.

People may disagree,

But RESPECT is to be maintained for free.

Grow your own friendship tree,

Stop blog-bullying from blocking your way.

## If All the Words Go Flat

If all the words go flat

Like the knap of a kitten's back,

Do you ruffle the page

2 show your waves of rage?

Do you Rally your courage

trying not to discourage?

Do you rabble up the rouse

2 insult someone's spouse?

Do you plant more pain

or figure out a way to explain?

Maybe you shall refrain

From emotional explosion,

I will try to remain in a position

Where I am nowhere

near

artificial fame,

man-made shame,

Luxurious repasts,

Hatred blasts,

Big bigotry,

Polluted factory….

I will lean back,

Take a deep breath,

www.ingramcontent.com/pod-product-compliance
Ingram Content Group UK Ltd.
Pitfield, Milton Keynes, MK11 3LW, UK
UKHW040558210726
13854UKWH00008B/1408

9 781257 110582